Complete Daily Planner

for Today's Active, Busy Woman

@ Journals and Notebooks

@ Journals & Notebooks

All Rights reserved. No part of this book may be reproduced or used in any way or form or by any means whether electronic or mechanical, this means that you cannot record or photocopy any material ideas or tips that are provided in this book.

Copyright 2016

Monday		Tuesday	
To Do:	Notes:	To Do:	Notes:

Wednesday		Thursday	
To Do:	Notes:	To Do:	Notes:

Stay Active. Be Productive!

Friday

To Do:
_____
_____
_____
_____
_____
_____
_____
_____
_____

Notes:

Saturday

To Do:
_____
_____
_____
_____
_____
_____
_____
_____
_____

Notes:

Sunday

To Do:
_____
_____
_____
_____
_____
_____
_____
_____
_____

Notes:

Stay Active. Be Productive!

Monday

To Do:

Notes:

Tuesday

To Do:

Notes:

Wednesday

To Do:

Notes:

Thursday

To Do:

Notes:

Stay Active. Be Productive!

Friday

To Do:

Notes:

Saturday

To Do:

Notes:

Sunday

To Do:

Notes:

*Stay Active.
Be Productive!*

Monday
To Do:

Notes:

Tuesday
To Do:

Notes:

Wednesday
To Do:

Notes:

Thursday
To Do:

Notes:

Stay Active. Be Productive!

Friday

To Do:

Notes:

Saturday

To Do:

Notes:

Sunday

To Do:

Notes:

Stay Active. Be Productive!

Monday

To Do:

Notes:

Tuesday

To Do:

Notes:

Wednesday

To Do:

Notes:

Thursday

To Do:

Notes:

Stay Active. Be Productive!

Friday

To Do:

Notes:

Saturday

To Do:

Notes:

Sunday

To Do:

Notes:

Stay Active. Be Productive!

Monday

To Do:

Notes:

Tuesday

To Do:

Notes:

Wednesday

To Do:

Notes:

Thursday

To Do:

Notes:

Stay Active. Be Productive!

Friday

To Do:

Notes:

Saturday

To Do:

Notes:

Sunday

To Do:

Notes:

Stay Active. Be Productive!

Monday
To Do:
Notes:

Tuesday
To Do:
Notes:

Wednesday
To Do:
Notes:

Thursday
To Do:
Notes:

Stay Active. Be Productive!

Friday

To Do:

Notes:

Saturday

To Do:

Notes:

Sunday

To Do:

Notes:

Stay Active. Be Productive!

Monday		Tuesday	
To Do:	Notes:	To Do:	Notes:

Wednesday		Thursday	
To Do:	Notes:	To Do:	Notes:

Stay Active. Be Productive!

Friday

To Do:

Notes:

Saturday

To Do:

Notes:

Sunday

To Do:

Notes:

Stay Active. Be Productive!

Monday
To Do:
_____
_____
_____
_____
_____
_____
_____
_____
_____

Notes:

Tuesday
To Do:
_____
_____
_____
_____
_____
_____
_____
_____
_____

Notes:

Wednesday
To Do:
_____
_____
_____
_____
_____
_____
_____
_____
_____

Notes:

Thursday
To Do:
_____
_____
_____
_____
_____
_____
_____
_____
_____

Notes:

_____
_____
_____
_____
_____
_____
_____

Stay Active. Be Productive!

Friday

To Do:

Notes:

Saturday

To Do:

Notes:

Sunday

To Do:

Notes:

Stay Active. Be Productive!

Monday

To Do:

Notes:

Tuesday

To Do:

Notes:

Wednesday

To Do:

Notes:

Thursday

To Do:

Notes:

Stay Active. Be Productive!

Friday

To Do:

Notes:

Saturday

To Do:

Notes:

Sunday

To Do:

Notes:

Stay Active. Be Productive!

Monday

To Do:

Notes:

Tuesday

To Do:

Notes:

Wednesday

To Do:

Notes:

Thursday

To Do:

Notes:

Stay Active. Be Productive!

Friday

To Do:

Notes:

Saturday

To Do:

Notes:

Sunday

To Do:

Notes:

Stay Active. Be Productive!

Monday

To Do:

Notes:

Tuesday

To Do:

Notes:

Wednesday

To Do:

Notes:

Thursday

To Do:

Notes:

Stay Active. Be Productive!

Friday

To Do:

Notes:

Saturday

To Do:

Notes:

Sunday

To Do:

Notes:

Stay Active. Be Productive!

Monday
To Do:

Notes:

Tuesday
To Do:

Notes:

Wednesday
To Do:

Notes:

Thursday
To Do:

Notes:

Stay Active. Be Productive!

Friday

To Do:

Notes:

Saturday

To Do:

Notes:

Sunday

To Do:

Notes:

Stay Active. Be Productive!

Monday

To Do:

Notes:

Tuesday

To Do:

Notes:

Wednesday

To Do:

Notes:

Thursday

To Do:

Notes:

Stay Active. Be Productive!

Friday

To Do:

Notes:

Saturday

To Do:

Notes:

Sunday

To Do:

Notes:

Stay Active. Be Productive!

Monday

To Do:

Notes:

Tuesday

To Do:

Notes:

Wednesday

To Do:

Notes:

Thursday

To Do:

Notes:

Stay Active. Be Productive!

Friday

To Do:

Notes:

Saturday

To Do:

Notes:

Sunday

To Do:

Notes:

*Stay Active.
Be
Productive!*

Monday

To Do:

Notes:

Tuesday

To Do:

Notes:

Wednesday

To Do:

Notes:

Thursday

To Do:

Notes:

Stay Active. Be Productive!

Friday

To Do:

Notes:

Saturday

To Do:

Notes:

Sunday

To Do:

Notes:

Stay Active. Be Productive!

Monday

To Do:

Notes:

Tuesday

To Do:

Notes:

Wednesday

To Do:

Notes:

Thursday

To Do:

Notes:

Stay Active. Be Productive!

Friday

To Do:

Notes:

Saturday

To Do:

Notes:

Sunday

To Do:

Notes:

Stay Active. Be Productive!

Monday

To Do:

Notes:

Tuesday

To Do:

Notes:

Wednesday

To Do:

Notes:

Thursday

To Do:

Notes:

Stay Active. Be Productive!

Friday

To Do:

Notes:

Saturday

To Do:

Notes:

Sunday

To Do:

Notes:

Stay Active. Be Productive!

Monday
To Do:
_____
_____
_____
_____
_____
_____
_____
_____
_____
_____

Notes:

Tuesday
To Do:
_____
_____
_____
_____
_____
_____
_____
_____
_____
_____

Notes:

Wednesday
To Do:
_____
_____
_____
_____
_____
_____
_____
_____
_____
_____

Notes:

Thursday
To Do:
_____
_____
_____
_____
_____
_____
_____
_____
_____
_____

Notes:

_____
_____
_____
_____
_____
_____
_____

Stay Active. Be Productive!

Friday

To Do:
_____
_____
_____
_____
_____
_____
_____
_____
_____
_____

Notes:

Saturday

To Do:
_____
_____
_____
_____
_____
_____
_____
_____
_____
_____

Notes:

Sunday

To Do:
_____
_____
_____
_____
_____
_____
_____
_____
_____
_____

Notes:

Stay Active. Be Productive!

Monday
To Do:

Notes:

Tuesday
To Do:

Notes:

Wednesday
To Do:

Notes:

Thursday
To Do:

Notes:

Stay Active. Be Productive!

Friday

To Do:

Notes:

Saturday

To Do:

Notes:

Sunday

To Do:

Notes:

Stay Active. Be Productive!

Monday
To Do:

Notes:

Tuesday
To Do:

Notes:

Wednesday
To Do:

Notes:

Thursday
To Do:

Notes:

Stay Active. Be Productive!

Friday

To Do:

Notes:

Saturday

To Do:

Notes:

Sunday

To Do:

Notes:

Stay Active. Be Productive!

Monday

To Do:

Notes:

Tuesday

To Do:

Notes:

Wednesday

To Do:

Notes:

Thursday

To Do:

Notes:

Stay Active. Be Productive!

Friday

To Do:

Notes:

Saturday

To Do:

Notes:

Sunday

To Do:

Notes:

Stay Active. Be Productive!

Monday

To Do:
_____
_____
_____
_____
_____
_____
_____
_____
_____

Notes:

Tuesday

To Do:
_____
_____
_____
_____
_____
_____
_____
_____
_____

Notes:

Wednesday

To Do:
_____
_____
_____
_____
_____
_____
_____
_____
_____

Notes:

Thursday

To Do:
_____
_____
_____
_____
_____
_____
_____
_____
_____

Notes:

_____
_____
_____
_____
_____
_____
_____

Stay Active. Be Productive!

Friday
To Do:
Notes:

Saturday
To Do:
Notes:

Sunday
To Do:
Notes:

Stay Active. Be Productive!

Monday

To Do:

Notes:

Tuesday

To Do:

Notes:

Wednesday

To Do:

Notes:

Thursday

To Do:

Notes:

Stay Active. Be Productive!

Friday

To Do:

Notes:

Saturday

To Do:

Notes:

Sunday

To Do:

Notes:

*Stay Active.
Be
Productive!*

Monday
To Do:

Notes:

Tuesday
To Do:

Notes:

Wednesday
To Do:

Notes:

Thursday
To Do:

Notes:

Stay Active. Be Productive!

Friday

To Do:

Notes:

Saturday

To Do:

Notes:

Sunday

To Do:

Notes:

Stay Active. Be Productive!

Monday
To Do: **Notes:**

Tuesday
To Do: **Notes:**

Wednesday
To Do: **Notes:**

Thursday
To Do: **Notes:**

Stay Active. Be Productive!

Friday

To Do:

Notes:

Saturday

To Do:

Notes:

Sunday

To Do:

Notes:

Stay Active. Be Productive!

Monday
To Do:

Notes:

Tuesday
To Do:

Notes:

Wednesday
To Do:

Notes:

Thursday
To Do:

Notes:

Stay Active. Be Productive!

Friday

To Do:

Notes:

Saturday

To Do:

Notes:

Sunday

To Do:

Notes:

Stay Active. Be Productive!

Monday

To Do:

Notes:

Tuesday

To Do:

Notes:

Wednesday

To Do:

Notes:

Thursday

To Do:

Notes:

Stay Active. Be Productive!

Friday

To Do:

Notes:

Saturday

To Do:

Notes:

Sunday

To Do:

Notes:

Stay Active. Be Productive!

Monday
To Do:

Notes:

Tuesday
To Do:

Notes:

Wednesday
To Do:

Notes:

Thursday
To Do:

Notes:

Stay Active. Be Productive!

Friday

To Do:

Notes:

Saturday

To Do:

Notes:

Sunday

To Do:

Notes:

Stay Active. Be Productive!

Monday
To Do:

Notes:

Tuesday
To Do:

Notes:

Wednesday
To Do:

Notes:

Thursday
To Do:

Notes:

Stay Active. Be Productive!

Friday
To Do:

Notes:

Saturday
To Do:

Notes:

Sunday
To Do:

Notes:

Stay Active. Be Productive!

Monday

To Do:

Notes:

Tuesday

To Do:

Notes:

Wednesday

To Do:

Notes:

Thursday

To Do:

Notes:

Stay Active. Be Productive!

Friday

To Do:

Notes:

Saturday

To Do:

Notes:

Sunday

To Do:

Notes:

Stay Active. Be Productive!

Monday

To Do:

Notes:

Tuesday

To Do:

Notes:

Wednesday

To Do:

Notes:

Thursday

To Do:

Notes:

Stay Active. Be Productive!

Friday

To Do:

Notes:

Saturday

To Do:

Notes:

Sunday

To Do:

Notes:

Stay Active. Be Productive!

Monday
To Do:
Notes:

Tuesday
To Do:
Notes:

Wednesday
To Do:
Notes:

Thursday
To Do:
Notes:

Stay Active. Be Productive!

Friday

To Do:

Notes:

Saturday

To Do:

Notes:

Sunday

To Do:

Notes:

Stay Active. Be Productive!

Monday

To Do:

Notes:

Tuesday

To Do:

Notes:

Wednesday

To Do:

Notes:

Thursday

To Do:

Notes:

Stay Active. Be Productive!

Friday

To Do:

Notes:

Saturday

To Do:

Notes:

Sunday

To Do:

Notes:

Stay Active. Be Productive!

Monday
To Do:
Notes:

Tuesday
To Do:
Notes:

Wednesday
To Do:
Notes:

Thursday
To Do:
Notes:

Stay Active. Be Productive!

Friday

To Do:

Notes:

Saturday

To Do:

Notes:

Sunday

To Do:

Notes:

Stay Active. Be Productive!

Monday

To Do:

Notes:

Tuesday

To Do:

Notes:

Wednesday

To Do:

Notes:

Thursday

To Do:

Notes:

Stay Active. Be Productive!

Friday

To Do:

Notes:

Saturday

To Do:

Notes:

Sunday

To Do:

Notes:

Stay Active. Be Productive!

Monday		Tuesday	
To Do :	Notes :	To Do :	Notes :

Wednesday		Thursday	
To Do :	Notes :	To Do :	Notes :

Stay Active. Be Productive!

Friday

To Do:

Notes:

Saturday

To Do:

Notes:

Sunday

To Do:

Notes:

Stay Active. Be Productive!

Monday

To Do:

Notes:

Tuesday

To Do:

Notes:

Wednesday

To Do:

Notes:

Thursday

To Do:

Notes:

Stay Active. Be Productive!

Friday

To Do:

Notes:

Saturday

To Do:

Notes:

Sunday

To Do:

Notes:

Stay Active. Be Productive!

Monday

To Do:
_____
_____
_____
_____
_____
_____
_____
_____

Notes:

Tuesday

To Do:
_____
_____
_____
_____
_____
_____
_____
_____

Notes:

Wednesday

To Do:
_____
_____
_____
_____
_____
_____
_____
_____

Notes:

Thursday

To Do:
_____
_____
_____
_____
_____
_____
_____
_____

Notes:

_____
_____
_____
_____
_____
_____

Stay Active. Be Productive!

Friday

To Do:

Notes:

Saturday

To Do:

Notes:

Sunday

To Do:

Notes:

Stay Active. Be Productive!

Monday

To Do:

Notes:

Tuesday

To Do:

Notes:

Wednesday

To Do:

Notes:

Thursday

To Do:

Notes:

Stay Active. Be Productive!

Friday

To Do:

Notes:

Saturday

To Do:

Notes:

Sunday

To Do:

Notes:

Stay Active.
Be
Productive!

Monday
To Do:
Notes:

Tuesday
To Do:
Notes:

Wednesday
To Do:
Notes:

Thursday
To Do:
Notes:

Stay Active. Be Productive!

Friday	
To Do:	Notes:

Saturday	
To Do:	Notes:

Sunday	
To Do:	Notes:

Stay Active.
Be
Productive!

Monday

To Do:

Notes:

Tuesday

To Do:

Notes:

Wednesday

To Do:

Notes:

Thursday

To Do:

Notes:

Stay Active. Be Productive!

Friday

To Do:

Notes:

Saturday

To Do:

Notes:

Sunday

To Do:

Notes:

Stay Active. Be Productive!

Monday
To Do:

Notes:

Tuesday
To Do:

Notes:

Wednesday
To Do:

Notes:

Thursday
To Do:

Notes:

Stay Active. Be Productive!

Friday

To Do:

Notes:

Saturday

To Do:

Notes:

Sunday

To Do:

Notes:

Stay Active. Be Productive!

Monday
To Do:

Notes:

Tuesday
To Do:

Notes:

Wednesday
To Do:

Notes:

Thursday
To Do:

Notes:

Stay Active. Be Productive!

Friday

To Do:

Notes:

Saturday

To Do:

Notes:

Sunday

To Do:

Notes:

Stay Active. Be Productive!

Monday

To Do:

Notes:

Tuesday

To Do:

Notes:

Wednesday

To Do:

Notes:

Thursday

To Do:

Notes:

Stay Active. Be Productive!

Friday	
To Do:	Notes:

Saturday	
To Do:	Notes:

Sunday	
To Do:	Notes:

Stay Active. Be Productive!

Monday
To Do:
_____
_____
_____
_____
_____
_____
_____
_____

Notes:

Tuesday
To Do:
_____
_____
_____
_____
_____
_____
_____
_____

Notes:

Wednesday
To Do:
_____
_____
_____
_____
_____
_____
_____
_____

Notes:

Thursday
To Do:
_____
_____
_____
_____
_____
_____
_____
_____

Notes:

_____
_____
_____
_____
_____
_____
_____

Stay Active. Be Productive!

Friday

To Do:

Notes:

Saturday

To Do:

Notes:

Sunday

To Do:

Notes:

Stay Active. Be Productive!

Monday

To Do:

Notes:

Tuesday

To Do:

Notes:

Wednesday

To Do:

Notes:

Thursday

To Do:

Notes:

Stay Active. Be Productive!

Friday

To Do:

Notes:

Saturday

To Do:

Notes:

Sunday

To Do:

Notes:

Stay Active. Be Productive!

Monday

To Do:

Notes:

Tuesday

To Do:

Notes:

Wednesday

To Do:

Notes:

Thursday

To Do:

Notes:

Stay Active. Be Productive!

Friday

To Do:

Notes:

Saturday

To Do:

Notes:

Sunday

To Do:

Notes:

Stay Active. Be Productive!

Monday

To Do:

Notes:

Tuesday

To Do:

Notes:

Wednesday

To Do:

Notes:

Thursday

To Do:

Notes:

Stay Active. Be Productive!

Friday
To Do:
Notes:

Saturday
To Do:
Notes:

Sunday
To Do:
Notes:

Stay Active. Be Productive!

Monday

To Do:

Notes:

Tuesday

To Do:

Notes:

Wednesday

To Do:

Notes:

Thursday

To Do:

Notes:

Stay Active. Be Productive!

Friday

To Do:

Notes:

Saturday

To Do:

Notes:

Sunday

To Do:

Notes:

Stay Active. Be Productive!

Monday

To Do:

Notes:

Tuesday

To Do:

Notes:

Wednesday

To Do:

Notes:

Thursday

To Do:

Notes:

Stay Active. Be Productive!

Friday

To Do:

Notes:

Saturday

To Do:

Notes:

Sunday

To Do:

Notes:

Stay Active. Be Productive!

Monday
To Do:

Notes:

Tuesday
To Do:

Notes:

Wednesday
To Do:

Notes:

Thursday
To Do:

Notes:

Stay Active. Be Productive!

Friday

To Do:

Notes:

Saturday

To Do:

Notes:

Sunday

To Do:

Notes:

Stay Active. Be Productive!

Monday
To Do:
Notes:

Tuesday
To Do:
Notes:

Wednesday
To Do:
Notes:

Thursday
To Do:
Notes:

Stay Active. Be Productive!

Friday

To Do:

Notes:

Saturday

To Do:

Notes:

Sunday

To Do:

Notes:

Stay Active. Be Productive!

www.ingramcontent.com/pod-product-compliance
Lightning Source LLC
Chambersburg PA
CBHW081438220526
45466CB00008B/2431